The Torment's

of the

Modest, Secluded Farm Life

The Torment's

of the

Modest, Secluded Farm Life

My book

By

Doris Anne Beaulieu

1stBooks - rev. 8/28/00

About the Book

The book is a true story of a young girl living a very modest, secluded country life in the 1950's, in the state of Maine. She starts by explaining how country folks lived life year after year. Filed with down-home stories and humor for a true picture of how life was in the country with only your eight siblings for playmates.

Then she take's you though the hard young working years. And then how she was tormented mental in all directions as she enters the real world. She just couldn't believe or understand the world and it's language being raised as she was in the country going to a catholic school.

This book will bring you heart warming laughter, and tears to your eyes. Hopefully you will gain a better and close understanding of the old country folks.

DEDICATION

This book is dedicated to Brenda Walters who was my gardened angle. She took me in under her wing when I was a stranger to her and open the world to me piece by piece, day by day. She took the time to get to know me and was there through all my pain and suffering and was there to pick me up and guild me when I thought I was going to lose my mind. She protected me from harm physically and mentally and gave so much of her time to me without wanting anything in return. She has been truly my saver of life.

CONTENTS

INTRODUCTION

This is a true story which is not meant to be taken likely by anyone. It took place in a small town in Maine. This book has been written to help parents understand that over-sheltering and too much modesty may end in tragedy in later years. The effect is irreversible.

The author speaks of how she was raised in a modest secluded country farm, with the heart breaking feeling of having to leave little Patrick behind. This is when her modest upbringing takes over her life only to leave her in another complete tragedy. She falls within herself from another lost, to the point of wanting to kidnap. Can she ever recover? Will she ever be free of the unknown?

CHAPTER ONE

THE REPETED YEARLY WORK OF THE

SECLUDED FARM LIFE

On the farm where I was raised, life was very simple. We'd garden in the spring, then came picking berry time. There was strawberry picking for winter jam. This was an all day process. We'd start the day by picking them, then pick the tails off them. There was mom right behind us with a measuring cup to see how much we had picked if it wasn't enough back we'd have to go. Then came scratchy burning raspberry time that always cause some argue on who would get up first to pick their share first. We use to get mon in the middle of it by getting her to wake us up first, which came when dad got up to go work in the woods at five. You see the first one up got the best spots, but none of us was happy about getting all scratch up even thou we did wear long pants and sleeves, it still burned when we washed up.

Once we had told mom that the place she wanted us to pick had no raspberries so it would put a stop to having to go there, but she'd only get upset with us. You see when the berries were picked mom would clean them and put them in quarts baskets and sell them at the vegetable stand for fifty cents. We'd get five cents for each quart sold which meant five cents more for school supplies we needed come September. But if they didn't sell that day, jam they became and no five cents.

One day big brother got an idea. He put poison ivy all over us. Mom and Dad took two of us to the doctor in the big city where I for one couldn't even open my eye's. Of course as kid's to us that only meant we'd be the first to get the wiping. We were all scared and thank GOD the doctor didn't know for sure what it was but treated it as poison ivy anyway. He was an old country doctor and it was only the second time he seen it, but we were all glad it put an end to picking there. Nothing much was growing there and we were tired of mom getting upset with us. Mom and Dad always felt it was the spraying of the power lines that did it. It may have been the reason for the raspberry dying off, but not for what we did.

Mom was very upset on the lost. You see, selling helped out alot to pay for the feed of the cattle, taxes, and lot's of seeds. Mom made all our clothes, mostly only in the wintertime.

Then came lots of time spent on our knees pulling weeds in the garden not only for our winter supply, but also to sell at the vegetable stand for our income of the farm. We always prayed for a good crop and planted plenty so we would never come up short on our supply.

If one didn't grow so good we canned extra in another to offset it. Mom and Dad walked the rows up and down while waiting for the plants to grow to see how they were coming up. They were always so careful on rotating the crop and spreading manure on the gardens to help guarantee a good crop. Dad was a lumberjack, so the only time he could help was on weekends. And, of course, the priest was very understanding about Dad working on Sunday when it was necessary.

Haying always came when fourth of July came around , so seeing fire works was very rare in our childhood just like going to the beach in the summer time very rare in deed. Haying time was the highlight time of the summer. The only time we could actually have some fun . You see some of us got to jump in the hay to tap it down so we could fit more in the barn. We had to watch ourselves so we wouldn't't hit our heads on the wooded beams and poor little sister Jane was, as we now it know as an allergy to the hay. She seem to break out alot, like she was allergic to the country.

If there was time between haying and pulling weed we did get to the beach. It seemed like it took forever to get there, but it was only eight miles away. I think even though it's alot to pack, Mom really enjoyed the break of being able to sit down for awhile, even though we were always asking for something. We didn't go enough to really learn to swim so for most of us nine kids it was just a time to play in the water and if we got there before others came we got to check the beach out to see if anyone left something behind the day before. That was the only time we got cool-aid, so of course, we asked often for some. Dad had a Small aluminum boat, so he and the older boys would take off fishing. The day had to have some benefits to it. Fish for Friday. We were very strong catholics. Mom was learning to be a nun in Canada before she met Dad. I don't even remember Mom going fishing I know she can't swim and she surely loves fish, but on the boat when we were kid's I don't ever remember that. But I surely remember

5

uncle Jerry and Dad boat racing and Dad's money being all wet that Mom place them on the windowsill to dry.

I bet that was one race Dad will never forget.

We spent a few days in the summer before our teenage years picking bottles on the side of the road and walk miles to town to cash them in for extra money. Of course bottles in them days were only two cents and it took alot to make a dollar. Sometimes we got tired and knocked on doors and said we were collecting for a bottle drive. It sure saved alot of leg work.

Right before school would start, Mom would make us each a few new outfits for the new school year which was hard to find the time with the selling of vegetables at the fruit stand. Sometime especially when more of us started school, it wouldn't be done till we were in school. All us kids went to a catholic school, and at times they wouldn't start the same day as public schools did. Mom learnt that fast and when we were to small to walk home Mom would have to call a cab from the big city to pick us up and take us home. But as we got older we did walk home. I really never understood why the bus driver never told us that when he pick us up. We always had to find out the hard way.

During late summer and when school started, we spent our time canning. The day would start by us pealing corn and of course our house work before going for the bus at seven-thirty. Then after school for the first two or so weeks in September we had the hard job of digging potatoes by hand, on our knees with just a board. We couldn't take the chance of a potato getting hurt. Taxes on the farm had to be paid and fifty pound bags of potatoes made fast income, not like vegetables by the pounds.

Our school work was behind alot then as we worked till dark and being raised French also put us behind. For some of us mostly us older ones, or in between ones, getting caught up was much to hard. School was a struggle.

7

Other then school and church, we looked forward to Sunday. We had relatives in the big city who thought it was super to visit the farm. So in the winter months they always came to visit. It was a lot of fun to hear all the stories our Aunts and Uncles would tell us about Dad when he was a kid. Mom's face would get red, and Dad would tell them not to give us kids any ideas.

But that was the fun of it all, and they keep on telling us more just the same. There was a little bit of wildness in Dad and I think he really did enjoy them telling us their version of him. Dad was very different then Mom when it came to punishing us. He always told us it was because we got caught. The best story was when they took cow manure and wrapped it up in newspaper, put it on city folks steps and set it on fire and rang the door bell. Of course, the people stepped on it to put it off. And you guessed it, the manure was all over their feet. Uncle Pete sure enjoyed giving us all the expressions of that. And you can be sure that where Dad was mostly raised in the city somewhat there was many stories to tell. From bails of hay tricks on farmers, to watch tricks on a string.

Mom was the strict one who always disciplined us, because Dad worked all day in the woods. Mom was brought up in a convent so our upbringing was very religious and strict. So you can see why she turned so red when the stories were being told. We were always polite and waited until Dad got on a debating mood with the company before we would work ourselves in there somewhere. Sunday always went by much too fast. You can see after listening to so many of those stories why some of Dads wildness rubbed of on my brothers, Glenn, Roger, and David Thought they would join in the fun. If Dad it, it must be fun. Only they tried it with snowballs.

It was a Sunday afternoon, which was lucky for them. We of course, had company and the boys decided to have some fun of their own. They went to the end of our long driveway which was surrounded by trees, down to the end. They hid behind the snowbank, and when cars went by they threw snowballs. They almost hit our cousin's car when they were about to turn up the driveway. I guess they didn't see it or never thought it would be them. Well, we all wondered where they went to, but we thought they went to town to buy some candy as they did quite often when company came over. We kid's were raised to be seen and not heard. We always felt Mom and Dad would never miss us kids when company was over. The rest of us always covered for them for we knew we would get some when they returned. We all got along just fine as we were our only playmates. There were a few neighbors but we were raised not to speak to them as it was bothering the neighbors. But this time our thoughts were wrong.

When we saw a man coming up the driveway with David, that only meant trouble. David was only six years old and didn't know any better then to run up his driveway when they hit the mans windshield with the snowball. David was scared and you could smell it when he went by us to go change his pants. Well, the man started to tell Dad they had broken his windshield so Dad asked to see the car as the man had walked David up. After that, Glenn and Roger came home and the man's windshield was not broken at all. That's when cousin Armond said "Well uncle Albert looks like the boy's have a little of you in them." Dad gave that laughing look and told the boys since they got caught they can go take the manure pile down and spread it in the fields. Of course that meant with the wheel barrel. They sure would have gotten more if cousin Armond hadn't spoken up.

Winter time was a break time for us but even thou we had some time to go sliding down the wooded trails there was work to be done which was harder in deep snow, like taking the trash a half mile away in the woods. But the trails we had threw the woods were very rough and curvy, but the challenging part of it all was to make it down the path without crashing into a tree. It was fun to have snow flying on your face. We ended the sliding with a few bruises and cuts on our lips but we sure had fun. That was our good Sunday fun in the winter. One thing we were always frightened of in the winter time was getting chapped lips. We used to get some hard lickings for it and with Roger having to tend to the cows, he always got it the worst. I don't know where that idea came from, must be something the nuns had put in Mom's head. Mom thought it was from kissing.

Mom sewed or knitted most of the winter. When we girls got older we also learned to sew and knit. This was great for me because I could make my own dresses a few inches higher then my knees. The girls all signed up for Home Economics in High School. We were sure to get a good grade and we could create our own style and colors. Dad got us girls an old singer sewing machine at an antique store. The man thought it was beyond repair but Dad knew it was in need of oil real bad that's all.

I even took the challenge of making a man's pair of pants. It came out with flying colors, but I'll never take a challenge like that again. The thought of knowing I could do it was enough for me.

Thanksgiving was always celebrated at night as hunting season was a big event for us in the country. Winter meat for us kids, Dad would always get his even thou he never ate it himself. Mom couldn't trick him and he'd sure get mad if she tried too. This was a time of year when we never seen much of the boys. We were always excited when dark came and they weren't back home. I would always run to get Dads lunch pail when he came home every night to see if it was heavy. That would mean the heart and liver was inside and he got his deer. Then we'd run to see what he got.

Christmas was always lots of fun for us all. Grandma (Dads Mom) joined us with her basket of fruit and nuts, the only time we got an orange and she made sure it was a big one. We'd all get sent up to bed for about three hours, then Dad would make noise like Santa on the roof top and ring the bells that always hung on the door. And with a few ho ho ho we were told to come down the stairs where we would have to wait for everyone who may have really fallen asleep to come down. Dad past each gift one at a time so we all could see the expression on their faces when we found out who got what. Most all the gifts were not wrapped so we would sit in anticipation of who would get what. The ones that were wrapped were the ones from our godparents. We all got something to wear home made and one or two toys or game. Then Mom had a table of food we could choice to eat or play with what we got for a few hours.

CHAPTER TWO

THE FIFTY - FIFTY HARD WORKING

TEENAGE YEARS

Our teenage years were busier than ever on the farm. In the summer time we would get working permits from the superintendent's office so we could get a job in order to buy our school clothes or material and things we needed for school. But first we had to give half of our pay to our parents, since we were not home to do our chores on the farm. I guess in a way it was paying room and board. Mom always packed our lunches and fixed us our oatmeal for breakfast when we got up. These lunches were different then the school lunches she would fix us of ketchup sandwich or molasses sandwich. We actually had lunch meat or peanut butter. Most of our lunch in the summer time was just tomatoes or bread and butter with a cucumber or a hand full of radishes and we worked hard for it too. We were raised you had to work for your meals and ate what was served to. Having cows on the farm meant you always got all the milk you wanted and that saved us from complete hunger often.

Mom also keep supper warm for me, since I worked in Yarmouth Fish Factory. That was over an hour ride for me and made the day long. I was picked up between five thirty and six in the morning and return about the same time at night. This is when we got to choice the color shoes we wanted from the Sears catalog. Finally get rid of those red shoes. Mom keep control and say so of our half but we always got to choice the color. I did so well on piece work at the fish factory that Dad did let me, and went with me to buy a cedar hope chest. Dad was good at getting a knock down price. Being such a small girl and short I made quite a hit with the boss. To begin with I needed a stool to reach the can on the top belt. And my way of packing was very different from the professional packers and everyone thought it was alright the way I did it. The boss used to tell me I was double handling the fish and could make more doing it his way. I never said anything, but I always thought it must be nice to be tall and to just turn around and grab the cans you needed.

One Saturday we had to work because one of the boats came in late. I never really cared to work on Saturday, but the money was extra good to have. There weren't too many workers who showed up, so the boss tried to keep us all going so we could leave as soon as possible. So when he stopped by my table he said, "let me show you how much more you can pack if you learn to do it my way," well I guess you know that got everyone going in the plant, and the race was on. Even the professional packers who won all those fast packing contests were teasing him that I may show him a better and faster way of doing things.

They always protected me from people who would come to visit the plant and always made comments of why I was packing the way I did. They always said leave the poor girl alone, she makes plenty on piece work, or if you can't beat her leave her be.

I always looked at the girls afterwards and smiled, I never got to know them too well, because they were always too busy making money to talk to anyone. The boss never gave them a hard time.

Being across from them helped me to learn speed which paid off the day of the race. Everyone kept walking by to see that the boss was quite a packer himself and cheering me on. I think they thought I needed it and boy they were right. In the first place I had never had to share my table with anyone before because of the way I packed, I needed it all for myself. He was really going fast at first and I was sweating it because I felt if he would win it meant I would have to do it his way. The faster packing girls would tease him often and always kept an eye on how the race was going. I think they also felt he may try to get me to change my way of packing if I lost. Well the boss and I got to know each other a little better that day. He began to see how short I really was and started to make comments on it. Shortness had everything to do with my way. I started to feel a little better that at least he was noticing that, and if I lost hopefully he would not have change my way of doing things. Thank GOD I won. The girls all enjoyed the fact that I shut him up. He no longer could say a thing about my packing anymore. They also asked him if they should change their way of packing. He was very nice about it and it sure made a lot of talk around the shop, and for the people who came to visit the plant. His wife also came in to congradulate me. I must have been the work talk that most men bring home. I thought it was great and he sure was a good sport. During the race he also took a lot of notice on the work I was putting out. On payday he would take me to the bank on our lunch break to make sure I would make it back on time and safely. We had to cash our check at lunch time because we got out too late on Friday and the banks would be closed. I really enjoyed the power of making money and the thought of spending half of it was thrilling enough. Never made nothing like this babysitting. I would buy plenty of material so in the winter I could sew myself some new dresses. Dad always told me to spend my money on clothes so I could be the best dress girl in town. The only time I remember getting a store bought dress was when the nuns in grammar school wanted me to dance at their fun raising bean suppers. Because I was so small and loved to dance they always used me when people came to visit the school or for raising money to keep the school open. Most of the catholic were big families and the schools ran on tuition which most couldn't afford much.

One other thing Dad always taught us if you don't have the cash you don't need it. So it was important to put money away for the winter for material, yarn or anything you might need for school.

School was where I meet my first love. It started when my girlfriend introduced him to me as her cousin. From there it was really nice, because he was always with me at recess and would walk me to my next class. One day I was sitting in the guidance office studying when I looked up from my book and there stood Howard. He really never talked too much, but he was always there. Then one day a teacher called a few of us students into his classroom because someone was ripping paperback books. We sometimes spent our recess in that room.

Since no one admitted to it, we were all punished by staying after school for a week.

School was just about three-fourth over when they had a record hop dance. I wanted to go to the dance with Howard but I couldn't seem to get in touch with him on such short notice, so I asked my Dad if he would take me to

21

the dance. Dad agreed, but he would always pick me up by ten the latest. My sister or brother would also have to agree to go with me. When sister Mary went with me she wouldn't make me pay her way, but when brother Roger went he would make me not only pay his way in, but also plenty for soda and chips. He never was cheap to take along. When I went to the dance I saw Howard there, but he only stayed to watch, not to dance. I paid to dance so when the music started I began to ask the guys if they wanted to dance. We danced for two hours, and just before the dance was over I tried to find Howard with no success.

The next day I found out why Howard had left the dance that night. Someone said he was a very shy person. His brother Neil sure made up for Howard's shyness. He was always up to something, and you never knew what he was going to do next. He was wild with the woman and always gave us lot's of laughs. Howard was a senior in High School, and was about to graduate when we finally got close. Howard had joined the Marine Corps while he was still in school and was to leave in July after he graduated. We had dated only a short time and then the school year was at an end. His mother Ellen planned a going away party for him. When she called me up to ask if I would like to come to the party, I said I would love to go but I had no way to get there and had no idea of where the name of the street was. She told me Howards brother Neil would pick me up by seven for the party. This was when I got to meet his mom and other members of his family. Ellen knew everyone in town, and was very stunned when her son told her he was dating. At first she couldn't believe he had a girl friend, because he was so shy, but to have a girl she knew nothing about surprised her even more. She didn't know us country folks. At the party we got to talk together which we didn't have time to do in school. The party was very well put together, and we had time to spend alone.

I hated to see the party come to an end. I wanted to spend more time with Howard, but it ended with us saying our goodbyes and we wished each other the best of luck in the future.

The next day Howard was off to South Carolina for boot camp. I was back to the fish factory for another summer. I felt bad about him leaving, knowing it would be a long time before we would spend time together again.

Work kept me very busy for the rest of the summer. We wrote to each other at least twice a week; but it still wasn't the same at all.

When school started a guy named Bill started to show me some interest. He use to see me at the coffee shop where I use to go before school started. My first class of the day was study hall so most of us in that class meet at the coffee shop almost across from school. He soon got the message I wasn't interest in him as anything more then a friend. He still always paid for my hot chocolate and donut.

Later that school year I was invited to the school prom by Jeff Walters who was from a wealthy family. He wanted me to meet his family before we went out. Mom made me a sparkling pink peach dress and fixed my long hair up. She use to help my aunt in the beauty salon in Canada, before she married Dad on occasions. I was dress to kill that night. Dancing of course came easy to me that night. My experience of my younger days in the Catholic school of dancing for every special events or fun raising project that came gave me a smooth rythum for dancing with a partner. The nuns always spoiled me rotten so I would dance for them. Most of the dresses I wore then were rented, but I always felt special in them. Tonight in this sparkling dress Mom made for me I felt that special feeling again. I felt so pampered that night at the prom. We all went to the Steak House for steaks after the prom. I really felt like a kid, I didn't know how to order or what to order since I never been inside a restaurant before in my life. And for someone else to be paying, it also made me feel strange inside. The prices were real high and I didn't know if he had such money, it just didn't feel right. The only steak we ever had was deer steak. I never thought it would taste like that did. The steak was so fatty. I dislike fat on my meat. We ended the night at about one in the morning. I had never had such a high class night. We courted for about a month, and he wanted me to go to every event he attended. But there was work to be done on the farm and he didn't like my saying "no" so often.

Howard was still writing even though I was dating other guys. We were still best of friends and we agreed when he came home on leave, we would get together and talk. One Friday night about seven-thirty, Howard's brother called me up to say Howard would be on the morning plane in Portland. I told Neil I would call him back later after I asked Dad if I could go meet him.

At home we always asked Mom if we could go and she would say to ask my father, then we'd ask him and he'd say to ask my mother. Well that would go back and forth for a while and after finding out who was to give permission, Mom then said, " I still had to do the dusting and wash the floors". So with the night almost over I first asked if I could call Neil to let him know I could go. He told me to be ready by seven in the morning. Well, that was much too early. I had to do my house cleaning before I could go anywhere , so I made a deal with my sister Mary to do my work on top of her own. She did of course because I paid her a price she liked. I was also glad to pay it. Mom didn't like it, but Dad said as long as the work Mom asked was done, it was O.K. So, Mary told Mom she needed the money for nylons for school. I got up early that morning so Neil could pick me up on time. Neil was a little late getting there, but he explained why he was late. He said, "I had a hard night." I never did ask him what he meant by that.

I soon learned how much of a lead foot Neil really was. I spent most of the time praying to get there safely. When we got to the airport the man on the intercom called out Neil's name and said he had a telephone call. It was his mother telling him that Howard had missed the plane and was coming by bus. So we called the bus station to find out what time his bus would be in. They told us not until noon or after. So Neil and I went to get some lunch, then to the bus station to wait for Howard. Meanwhile, Neil had fallen asleep in the chair while waiting. I felt very uneasy when he started to snore his head off. An hour and a half had passed by the time the lady came on the intercom saying the bus which Howard was on had arrived. I was glad to interrupt Neil's snoring to let him know.

It was almost two in the afternoon when we finally met. We wouldn't have much time together, his plane back was in the morning. We made the most of the time we had and decided to go steady again. As time went by, we continued to write and Howard came on weekends as often as he could.

When Howard got out of boot camp he tried to let me know he was home for a few weeks. This was around Christmas time and he came up to the farm to give me a Christmas present. He knocked at the front door and Mom answered it. He asked if I was home, and Mom told him that I wasn't and that I was baby sitting for the night. Only because she had heard a few stories about Howards family is why she said this. She then gave me the present that he bought me for christmas. I was happy to get it because I didn't't know he was home.

The next day I tried to call him, but every time I would try he wasn't't at home. Next thing I knew he had gone back. Within a few day's I received a letter saying he was sorry he had missed me when he was home. We still kept writing to each other twice a week. One day I told everyone at school that I had received a letter from him and that he would be coming home in about five weeks. I just couldn't wait to see him, and was glad that it would be for a week. When he arrived we went out to eat at a nice restaurant. He then had to go back, but this time he was going to North Carolina to learn to drive trucks. I think I received one letter before Howard's mom called me up to say that she received a set of wedding rings. When Howard came home on his April weekend he proposed to me. We then set a date and time on when we would get married. The date was in August of the same year. That night Howard was going to ask my Dad for my hand in marriage, but I told him that was too old fashioned, but he still came over. I told him to let me handle telling them . I never told Howard what Mom had said or how she felt to spare him hurt feelings. Being the shy guy he was it didn't take to much talking to change his mind and let me do it my way.

The next day while I was washing my long hair I told Mom. Her first words were " to who". I guess because she had disapproved of the family, she must of thought I moved on to someone else. When I told her she thought it was to soon, not giving them enough time to do everything. Dad always had a good sense of humor teasing me on how in his days when the man asked for the daughter's hand the groom had to give the brides father an animal in exchange. The groom would then receive one from the father. I told Dad he was going to ask you for my hand, but I talked him out of it.

Time for Mom to get ready for my wedding came even sooner. When Howard returned to base he was told that he was one they had picked to go to Hawaii. The stay there was to be for two years. He was to report to base in the middle of July.

Mom now had to work on my dress and veil even faster. She also had to make the bridesmaid's dress too.

The hardest time we had was to find a size five two inch heel shoe. We went to the big city and even walked in some fancy shoe stores only to hear them say they didn't carry heeled shoes for kids. I felt like telling them a few things. Mom gave me a shower and my Aunt Theresa who worked in a shoe factory gave me the pair she had on her feet. She also was very short and had the same problem I had, but the factory always made small shoes for display. When the factory change the styles, they would give the sample to my aunt, since she worked there. All the relatives knew we were going to Hawaii, so gifts were light-weight items or money which really came in handy later on. The wedding was held in our small town church were we been all our life and with the same priest. So with all the relatives the church was filled. There were all sorts of different colorful flowers and a white carpet to walk down the aisle on. Howard was dressed in his Marine Corp dress blues and he really looked great. Blue was a nice color for his eyes. When the ceremony was over they all started throwing rice and confetti at us all the way to the car. We rode around town blowing horns and then to the hall where the reception was held. The reception was always full of surprises in this family. Since it was the first wedding Mom and Dad were giving, they went all out and everyone really raised some hell. This was the first time so many relatives have been together in a long time. My godfather grabbed me and started going out the back door with me on his shoulders. Just then Howard, not knowing how much of a joker he was, said "hey, bring her back here. She's my baby now!" everyone loved that one.

Our honeymoon was spent in the hotel in Brunswick, Maine. Where for the first time in days I went to bed before midnight. Well, what a night that was. The first thing we did was order something to eat. After that we just couldn't figure out what to do he was just as shy as I was.

On Monday we went to the Naval Air Station to get my I.D. card made out. Then we went to the Social Security Office to get my card change to my married name. Howard dropped me off at the farm and went to make the reservation for us to fly to Hawaii. Everyone thought Hawaii was a wonderful honeymoon place. I thought so, too.

CHAPTER THREE

THE TRAGEDY OF LEAVING LITTLE

PATRICK BEHIND

I had never been away from home and the thought of leaving was really frightening, but I tried very hard to accept it. We were to leave in the morning on a large plane which I had never been on before, it was a strange feeling for me. When night came I went back to the farm to say goodbye to everyone. My little brother Patrick and I walked up the field to the garden where the sounds of the night always had you at peace. You could hear the frogs crock and the sound of the water running down over the rocks, that's such a peaceful sound. I had been so busy with my wedding I had never even helped with the planting of the garden. Patrick, who was only seven, showed me the spot where he had planted his own special garden. Then as we walked I thought of all the time I rocked little Patrick. By the time Mom had Little Patrick Dad was at the point were he was tired more at night from working all day in the woods, that at night he needed to sleep so hearing a baby cry was not what he needed to here. So Mom put him and his crib in my room .I also couldn't handle hearing him cry so as soon as Mom got to the bottom of the steps I would take him and put him in bed with me. Sometimes he wouldn't let Mom get to the bottom and he'd start saying "do do" he was just learning to talk and called me that. Mom was always so busy that when ever Patrick got hurt I was the one to take care of him.

The walk back to the house became quite as I just didn't know how to tell Patrick I would be gone for a long time. Just then Patrick picked up a wild flower and gave it to me. That's when I began to cry. I didn't want to leave him behind. To think I wouldn't see him for two years it was just too much for me to take. Patrick and I were so close, even with such an age difference. Even when he was ill I was the one who took care of him. Like the time grandma came to visit for the weekend, she was showing David how to clear bushes so he could build a tent. They were using tree cutter, and Patrick had gotten in the way and had his toe cut. We were in the country and Dad was not home from work yet. We kids never went to the doctor since money was always a problem.

I was the one to try to keep him from crying and cuddle him at the same time. Grandma was trying to use some old time remedy by wrapping his toe in mud and some leaves. Mom was very upset over it. She washed out the mud because she was afraid of infection setting in. Mom was in the middle of something. I can't remember what, then she had to get supper ready before Dad got home. Dad always had to have supper ready when he arrived home, though it meant the rest of us waiting for an hour or two. Anyway, Patrick was always very comfortable with me and asked if I could rock him. He was only about two at the time. When Patrick was put into the boys room at about five to sleep, Mom would check on him before going to bed when he was ill. At first when she couldn't find him she'd be checking under the beds, then she would often find him in bed with us girls.

When Patrick started kindergarten, he went in the morning to noon. Due to the over crowding in the high school I only went from seven in the morning till noon too. When it was the muddy season Dad couldn't work so he would take Patrick and I fishing in the afternoon.

So you see, Leaving him hurt so much. I found myself doubting why I had gotten married. When I used to come home from waitressing he would always run to the car to greet me, because I always gave him the small change. He would always put it in his piggy bank and he had more money in it then I had in the bank. I had him so used to getting his bank that when company came over he would pass his bank around for more. It was really funny.

When we got back to the house to say goodbyes to the rest of the family I saw Howard standing there. It made me feel a little better, because he knew how close we were. It was noticed by everyone who ever saw us together. Howard tried to at least dry my tears before we went into the house. The air was very quit and none of us could say too much since we were all so afraid we'd start to cry. Mom gave me some car sickness pills for the ride in the morning. I don't know where she got them unless she got them over the counter in the drug store. Mom always got car sick when going anywhere. Well, all I wanted to do was to go back to my older sisters house and go to bed and cry. So I said, "well it's time we were going." So we all just gave each other hugs and cried then we left. Howard drove around in silence for quite awhile before he asked me if I was alright. I felt totally wiped out and just wanted to sleep.

In the morning I called the farm once more. Howard's mother was there to take us to the airport, so now it was time to say goodbye to my sister. She had already shared last night's experience with me. So all we could do was to hug each other and promise to call just as soon as I got there. I don't think Howard's mother understood what was going on, but I didn't really care. She never said a thing, but I felt she thought it was silly. She didn't know how close we were all brought up to be. I also felt I was leaving security to go into the unknown. I had absolutely no idea what married life was or where we were going to stay, or what we were going to do. I didn't know anything about the service and didn't know what I was going to do when we arrived in Hawaii.

We were to spend four days in California while waiting for Howard's military plane to Hawaii. I was to take a regular flight out. I was scared at first on the plane, and took Mom's car sick pills, but all that did was to make me sleep. I had begun to enjoy watching what looked like snow covered mountains. It was so pretty. When we were coming down some of the states looked like a big housing project, with all kinds of toy cars and trucks to play with in a sandbox. Patrick would have had lots of fun with this one. Back home we had a sand pile, He used to enjoy pretending all kinds of silly things when he was playing with his trucks in it. As soon as we got to California I let Patrick know all about it. During our stay there we talked all our hurt feelings out, about how I hated leaving him behind. The brief stay gave me a chance to send out all those thank you cards for our wedding gifts. I didn't like taking the rest of the plane ride alone, But Howard's mother had given me a number to call when I arrived in Hawaii. It was of people she knew that were stationed there, I was to call them as soon as I arrived. Howard also spent a lot of time telling me it was going to be alright. There were no stops on the way so I should have no trouble. He also saw me off at the airport before going on his way.

CHAPTER FOUR

THE NIEVE ENTRY OF THE UNKNOWN

When I arrived in Hawaii is when I began to feel real lost. The number I was to call was only giving me a recording. I didn't know what to do when I turned around and a man kept looking at me. I quest it was easy to see I looked lost. I tried not to look at anyone, in hopes no one would notice me. I put my luggage in storage, then sat down to try to think of what I was going to do next. I didn't know what I should do, since Howard and I never talked about what I should do if things went wrong, or how he would know where I was or how to reach me. Since I didn't know anything about service life. I didn't know how to get in touch with him. I then thought of looking in the telephone book in case we may have wrote down the number wrong. ("Boy you should see the telephone books there"). I had trouble even handling it. Well I finally got the right people.

When Sue answered the phone, I introduced myself and told her who told me to call. She sounded a little surprised, and her husband was not home yet but gave me the address to take a cab. So I took my luggage and went on my way to take a cab. I had no idea how long it would take me to get there, but my eyes were really big, as the price per minute kept going up and up even when we stopped at a light. Back home lights were only in the really big city, so I never saw them very often. I wanted to jump out and change the light, because it was costing me more then I ever thought. I had no idea how much more we had to go.

Then we pulled in front of this great big building, the cab stopped and there stood Sue and her husband. They introduced themselves and welcomed me to the island. We went up in an elevator which really felt funny and dizzy to me. I found myself holding on to the sides without thinking. When I thought of it, I hope no one would think I was silly but I sure felt like falling. I held on tightly when it stopped on the different floors, for it was putting pressure in my head, and wouldn't you know it, they lived on the top floor.

While eating supper we talked about the flight over. I think that's when they realized they had a modest one on their hands. They then explained to me that sometimes when people like us come over the way we did they don't meet up for weeks. I was still welcome to stay with them. Sue said I would be company to talk to. Then we decided to go visit the mall. Well I went to get dressed after the dishes were done. When I came out they really had a good laugh and explained to me that I was going to see how the life style was very different there. People out here go shopping in their bathing suits. I found that to be embarrassing and hard to believe. Back home we always dressed up to go shopping.

They were sure right about that. I bet my face was red most of the time while we were shopping. When we first arrived at the parking lot I couldn't believe how big the place was. Rick, Sue's husband said there were ninety some odd stores. It was hard to believe so many stores all in one place, plus a parking building too. Well, now I though I just may like living here when I saw how many short people there were. It was mostly the Japanese people. My neck was finally going to get a break. The style of material was bright and cheerful to look at, and I decided to send some home to Mary as soon as I was settled in my own place. I didn't dare spend any money yet, but it was nice to see, all the beautiful material in such bright colors.

When we went home and time for bed came. I found myself not being able to sleep. All I kept on thinking was what Rick had said at supper time about Howard and I maybe never meeting up for weeks or more. I kept on hoping the phone would ring. After all, Howard was supposed to leave California three hours after me. I've been here ten hours now and no calls. Rick had also told me the service was not always on time, and it was possible he hadn't even left California yet. He didn't want me to get my hopes up.

At two o'clock in the morning the telephone started to ring. I automatically got up to answer it without even stopping to think it wasn't my home. Lucky enough it was my Howard and he was at the air base, I was filled with joy to hear his voice. I then heard the phone in the other room being picked up. It was Rick, he asked Howard which base he was on and where on the base he was at. Then he told him to stay put until we got there.

That night I slept peaceful, the worry of the trip was over now. All we had to do was to get our own place. Howard would go to work and all the confusion would be cleared at last.

We spent the weekend looking at the rent adds. Rick drove us to the other side of the island where Howard was to be stationed to check the paper there. We had no luck at all. There were no one bedroom furnished apartments. Rick told us that sometimes when landlords have apartments available they would list them with the base. Some felt better renting to military people because they'd always get their money, all they do is call your Commanding Officer, if there was a problem. Well, I didn't really understand what all that meant but it sounded alright to me.

Monday came and Howard had to go check in on base. He had to take the bus in order to get there. I really didn't feel right staying with Sue, I didn't know anything about her, and didn't know what we would talk about, so I decided to go with Howard that morning.

Howard tried to explain some of the military rules to me on the way over. When we got there I followed him into the barracks. With all those men around I stayed very close to Howard at all times. I followed him up the stairs, then all of a sudden things became very quite. An officer asked me to join him for a cup of coffee. I had no idea where Howard had gone. I really didn't like coffee at all but I didn't feel it was polite to say no to him. I thought Howard was going to be right back. He did say he only had to sign in and get some shots now that he was on the island but it took longer.

The officer asked about my trip over, then asked me what rank my husband was. He left the office and said he'd be right back. When he returned, he introduced me to another officer who was to show me around the base. So off we went. First he showed me where the exchange was in case I needed medical assistance. We then stopped at the snack shop for a soda and salad. He told me he was ordered to have a talk with me about money. Usually privates never bring their wives to Hawaii, because the pay wasn't enough to live on, they said. If we had financial problems, Uncle Sam would send me home. Well, we had plenty of money on hand, since most of the relatives gave us money as a wedding gift. I then asked him about what Rick had said to us about landlords calling in apartments. He told me it was so, and the base had set up the system to help families. This way they could get settled in faster and save the family a lot of money in hotel expenses. Before we went back to the office he showed me where it was located. He explained the first day of checking in was the longest. I began to look through the cards on file for a one bedroom apartment. I found one that seemed to be the lowest price one on file. Then I asked the girl if the apartments were nice. She assured me they were very neat apartments. The landlords said all appliances were in working order. I called the landlord up and asked if the apartment was rented, since it wasn't, we made an appointment for the next day. I then went to the exchange to pick up an alarm clock, then off to where Howard had gone to check in, but he wasn't ready yet. I decided to sit on the grass to wait for him. It was so funny to see how different the grass was then back home, or the grass we saw in California. It had a different shade to it. It took a long time before Howard came out and told me what had taken place while we waited at the bus stop. We were both glad at the thought of having our own place. We had been married two weeks now and really wanted to be alone for a change. We went back to Sue and Ricks and told them the good news. They were glad we had luck finding a place. I could see Sue was hoping we would stay with them longer, I guess she was homesick and us being there helped fill that spot for her. They had only been on the island a short time themselves. And really hadn't made any friends yet. We were moving on the other side of the island, which made it hard to travel back to the other side to see them again. We did get the apartment the next day and paid two months

51

rent and deposit. It was a good thing I did, since Uncle Sam took some time to begin paying Howard for living off base, Plus for being married. We moved that night which was easy, because all our things were in suit cases. We walked down to the store for some food and felt a little chilly. That evening I tried to turn up the heat, but found no controls. That seemed so funny to see no heaters around the floors. Back home we had a big wood furnace down in the basement, and I knew in the apartments in town they had registers but here I couldn't find anything. I sure learned from the hot day's that it definitely wasn't needed at all. The apartment was a kitchen living room combination, with a separate bedroom and bath. It had lovely apple green walls with bright flowered curtains, certainly a very neat cossy place for two.

The next morning Howard had to leave early, so I got up at five like Mom always did for Dad to cook his breakfast. It was my first meal I had ever cooked, so all had to be just right. I cooked eggs and ham and cut the ham up like Mom always did and buttered his toast. I woke Howard up after heating the hot water for coffee. When Howard came in the kitchen and saw what I did he busted out laughing. I felt maybe I cooked what he didn't like so I asked him what he wanted me to fix instead. He then apologized for laughing and said he didn't eat breakfast and that coffee would be just fine. He kept on staring at the breakfast. When I asked him what was so funny he asked me if I was going to cut up the meat for him all the time. I really didn't understand what he meant. Well, I found out after that Mom was the only one who had done that. Then he told me I was cute and left for work because he had to hitch a ride there.

I started cleaning the house after eating the breakfast, and found myself finished in no time at all. It seemed strange, because on the farm there was always work to be done. When we had nothing to do Mom always found some work for us. So I sat down and wrote to everyone back home. As I went to the mail box to put my letter in another girl was sitting on the steps waiting for the mailman. I started back upstairs and the girl asked me how I liked the apartment. She then asked if we were in the service. Then we started to talk about that. Brenda, who lived right under us, asked what rank my husband was. When I told her she looked strange. I then told her that I was told all about money yesterday. She then asked if my husband had put in papers for being married. I didn't know and would find out that night. When Howard came home, I asked him if he had put in the papers, and he did. After supper we went for a walk, and did some window shopping, except for one little gift we just had to buy for Patrick. The sun that night was so beautiful to see as it was going down. The air felt so calm and peaceful and I started to feel homesick again. For a week we spent our nights playing cards, or we'd go window shopping. We had no television or radio and playing cards helped pass the time by.

Once as I was waiting for the mailman Brenda asked me if we had a television. When I said no, she said she though so. She knew it was too quite where we lived. She then invited me to watch soap operas with her. I really thought watching a program that didn't end that day was silly. Back home T.V. was never put on until four-thirty, except on Saturday morning for the little ones to watch while the older ones cleaned the house.

CHAPTER FIVE

MODESTY OVERTOOK AND TOOK MY BABY "I WANT YOURS."

Brenda was four months pregnant at the time, and when she started to talk about it I turned red instantly. She then started to ask me about my home life, then apologized for the way she was talking. It's not that she used any bad language, but talked so openly about sex. In our home, harsh language was never spoken, and sex was thought of as being something bad and was never talked about. It took a lot out of Mom to explain what a Kotex was to us, and she never explained why or what was happening. At first I though I got hurt, but as time went on I found out the other girls at school had it too, and the nuns explained it a little bit more then Mom did. The rest was on our own.

So Brenda then invited Howard and I to supper. While setting up for supper we found out Brenda's husband was in the same platoon as Howard, so they started riding together. It really helped us out, because we didn't have to get up so soon. Brenda and I became real close, she was trying to fill me in on military life, and on life in general. I've gone through a lot of red faces, because I didn't know what the world was like and didn't understand alot of words she was using meant. I did however find what she was saying to be very interesting. Half the things she told me seemed unreal, and I began to think she had seen too many of those soap operas.

A month or so later, I told Brenda I thought I may be pregnant because I was two weeks late on my period. She then asked me if I had my medical cards. I didn't exactly know what she meant, but since I knew nothing about it I said no. She told me she would take me tomorrow to apply for one. Then told me what I needed to take with me for information. In the morning I felt a little light headed and sick to my stomach. I kept trying to tell myself it was only to fill in the papers. Brenda also gave me a cup for my first morning urine. When Brenda came up I told her I wasn't feeling well and didn't want to go. But she could see right through me and said I was going and there was nothing to be scared about. I didn't tell her how scared I was of doctors, because I really felt foolish enough already. When we arrived the place was crowed, which confused me. We had to get in line and Brenda had already told me what they were going to say. When my turn came up I could feel my face burning up and turned to Brenda. I was sure glad she stayed by my side, it made me feel much better when she took over for me. The lady's vocabulary threw me off. I didn't understand what she was asking and felt very embarrassed when answering them. The lady gave a slip for the lab, and Brenda said she knew where it was and took me there. We started down the hall, where all I kept seeing were doctors and nurses coming from all directions. I guess that's when I passed out, because the next thing I remember was Brenda putting a cold paper towel on my forehead. Brenda told me to lay there for awhile, she took my urine sample to the lab, thank God for plastic bottles.

When she returned we went out to eat at the snack bar, it was really great to have a friend like her. I was disappointed when the result came out negative. Brenda explained to me that it takes time before the test would come out positive, and that in two weeks we would take in another one. As we continued to watch soap operas together, I was learning more about the world around me. Brenda was having a party to celebrate her husbands new rank, and had invited Howard and I down. We still didn't have a television, so we thought it would be exciting to go. As it turned out we didn't stay very long, because the language the guys spoke was more then I could handle. I felt they were just awful to be talking that way. My face had been red and burning so often that I began getting lots of pressure in my head, that I was losing my hearing. When we went back upstairs, Howard felt hurt and told me people talk that way, and I was to be a military wife I best get used to it now. We went back after I calmed down. I still didn't like it, and my eyes got watery often and I made a lot of stops in the restroom. I was glad when the night came to an end.

The time came for me to take another urine test. It was a bit easier this time, at least I didn't pass out. The test was positive, and I jumped for joy. The thought of having a little one inside me felt great. I called Mom immediately to tell her the good news. She congratulated me and was happy.

I started to fix a special supper to celebrate the good news, while doing so I got confused in my thoughts. We were brought up that sex was bad, but yet I was happy about being pregnant, and felt confused; like everyone knew what I had done. I went down to talk to Brenda about it before Howard got home. She told me I should forget the thought of being bad, because it was a beautiful thing between two people, and to enjoy bringing a new life into the world. Well, now I was on cloud nine, so I went up to be sure everything was O.K. for supper. Howard knew something was up when he saw the flowers I picked outside on the table. He called his mom immediately and she was already telling us it was a girl. She had five boys and wanted a girl in the family real bad.

I told her it was traditional to have a boy first, so big brother would look after little sister. She said no way and we laughed about it. She then wanted to name the girl Lisa, I told her she could name her anything she wanted because I was having a boy. She wouldn't give in an inch, but managed to say as long as it's healthy, that all that counts. We felt so much closer that night, and talked how we were going to bring the child up. But I still insisted on having a boy first.

The next day Howard was all busy tailed when he woke up and told me to stay in bed instead of getting up. When I went to get the mail I stopped at Brenda's to tell her about what Howard's mom had said. She asked me if I had set up my doctor's appointment. Then she explained the test they would do, I began to get scared of the thought of them taking blood and a complete physical. Back home the only time I had a somewhat physical without blood work and without taking off all my clothes was when we entered high school. The school had to take us to the doctor because my Dad didn't have the time or money. But there were shots we had to have to enter High School.

I tried not to think of it as time came closer. I began to get a weird feeling and I refused to pass out this time. When Howard came home I told him of my fears, then asked him if I could do like Mom always did when it was time. She would go to the hospital and forget all those doctors visit Brenda had spoke about. With Mom we never knew she was pregnant until we woke up and saw a note on the wall. Grandma would be there when we got home from school, then she would take care of us until Mom came back home. My oldest sister Lisa was the one to fix us breakfast, and get us off to school, then wait for grandma to arrive. Lisa always got to stay home while Mom was away, because we were a little more than my grandma could handle, house work and all.

Howard said that there was no way I should do such a thing, especially when our medical help was free. This way we would be sure that the baby was alright. He had a lot of hang ups on the subject of prenatal care, because he had three brothers who were born handicapped. The first one died at nine months and two others were learning to deal with life and become responsible adults. So he did have a good reason to feel that way. I didn't know that much about their condition at the time, but they were different, and very lovable boys with special talent we always took for granted.

Howard went down to talk to Brenda to tell her of my uncertainties. Brenda then came up and asked if I wanted to go do some wash with her. I agreed, and when we got our wash in the washers we went for a soda. She told me what Howard had said about the way I felt. I felt a little better when she said everyone goes through it, and everything ends up alright. She also said that there was nothing to worry about, because she was going with me to the doctor.

I ate a good breakfast the next morning, when we arrived, all you could see were pregnant woman. I thought there would never be so many pregnant women in the world at the same time. I was handed a Johnny as they call it, to put on. I felt strange walking into the waiting room with nothing under my Johnny but bare skin. Brenda had saved me a seat. As we waited for my turn, which seemed like forever, I began feeling nervous. Hearing what the other ladies were saying, what the doctors were going to do to them, and how the labor was like in their other pregnancies, I soon found myself going to the bathroom often. It seemed like my turn was never going to come. An hour had passed and I was still waiting. My visits to the restroom began to be many and I had started to bleed. I was scared I had done something wrong, But I didn't dare to tell anyone. About ten minutes my name came up, and walking down the hall I thought the doctor was going to give me hell.

I went in and the doctor started to ask questions. I felt shaky answering them. I tried not to cry when he began to examine me, but I couldn't hold it. He had two nurse there to hold my knees so he could examine me. He tried to make conversation with me but the pressure in my head was blocking my hearing. All I could think of was the awful things they were doing to me. I guess he didn't notice I was bleeding and I was too scared to say anything. After I went home, I cried myself to sleep. When Howard came home I was still sleeping and then he woke me up and asked how the appointment went.

That night I just couldn't sleep, my stomach just kept on turning over and over again. I was still bleeding and was getting scared. I asked Howard to stay home that next day, but he told me he couldn't stay home through my whole pregnancy because Uncle Sam wouldn't allow it. Brenda kept the car for the day, and I spent the day in bed. When night came things weren't any better, so we called the hospital and were told to come in right away.

I was feeling so bad that the thought of being examined hadn't entered my mind. On the way to the other side of the island where the Army hospital was, I began to flow even faster and was getting weaker and sleepy. The doctor examined me right away, then put me in a wheelchair and said I was still young and could still have more children. I knew then I was going to lose the baby. When I arrived to my room they tried to put an I.V. in but was unsuccessedful after four times. All their poking had me in tears even more. My roommate's husband tried to cheer me up by saying there may be a steak dinner in there. I was in no mood to hear anything from anyone, so I said in that case you can have it. The doctor came in and tried to get the I.V. in and was successful that time. My veins were quite small then, so that was my problem. They kept examine me throughout the night. The last one of the night they thought they might have to abort the baby because I was losing too much blood. When Brenda came to visit the next day I asked her what all those words I was hearing meant. I found out what they meant and also what my blood type was. I had RH due negative. She then explained I would get a shot with a card I should keep in my purse at all times.

Howard's visit was a quiet one, and he didn't have much to say You could see he was hurt, but in the Marine Corps you are supposed to be tough. He never talked about how he felt and his visits were always short. I wanted to go home to Patrick and just hold him so I could have something I lost back. My roommate was in there to have her tubes tied and I just couldn't see how anyone could do such a thing like that. She made me so angry, I tried not to make any conversation with her at all. She went home the day after and I was glad. Now I wouldn't have to hear her talk to all the kids on the phone, one at a time. I just couldn't stomach it anymore.

Three days went by and when they came in to give me my shot it hit me that I had already lost my baby. I felt like hiding in a corner where no one could see me. When I went home I had to take it easy for awhile.

Weeks went by and the only time I went out was to get the mail. The thought of everyone knowing I was pregnant and the fact of losing the baby was too much for me to accept. Half of me seemed to be missing and Howard didn't seem so close anymore. Talk was very limited and we didn't want to do anything together. Somehow he was blaming me because I let my fears get the best of me. Many things that were said still didn't add up to me. I began to get angry with myself for not learning more English in school. Back home in school reading and English were the worst subjects for me. With all the farm work we had to do to survive, there was limited time for such things. But yet we were still expected to have passing grades which sometimes couldn't be done. Roger and I were the ones that had the most trouble learning. I don't blame Mom for not giving us extra time for study, where we had the problem. I believe she didn't know there was such a thing as a learning disability. There was no test in those days and the nuns had never suggested it. That was never heard of and even if it were, Mom would have never admitted it. To her we were just to lazy to learn. Mom couldn't read English then, so no one could help us except in French.

Brenda came over to give some books, she had picked up on her visit to the doctor. She said it may help me to understand what was taking place, and it would help me in the future, and not to take any of it personal.

We started to go out again only to find out that Howard had not told anyone at work of our loss. All they kept asking was how the baby doing. Thank God Brenda took over at that point. We later talked and she explained to me that Howard must be hurt inside, not to have told anyone what had happened. Howard and I had a long talk about it that night.

He said he had felt his manhood had been struck, and that we didn't have much time to enjoy anything. We had the joy for only two weeks. It seemed like everyone around me was having babies. When Howard and I would walk down the street and I would see a baby, Howard would just hold me tight and say we'd have one someday. I told him I wanted one now. The days seemed so empty to me with nothing to do.

Brenda had a girl and she was so beautiful. I use to go over and hold her and rock her to sleep. Every time I did this I would wish she was mine. It wasn't until the time Brenda had a cocktail party that she noticed how attached I was with her baby. She then took the baby from me and put her to bed for the night.

The next day she got the neighbor to babysit and came over to talk to me. She was very open with me and she was right. I told her how hard it was for me to walk down the street and stop myself from thinking of stealing a baby. She understood my hurt and we talked so many times about it. When she started to work she asked me to babysit and of course I was delighted. She also gave me many activities to do so I wouldn't have much time to think about

my lose.

CHAPTER SIX

" NO" DON'T LET IT HAPPEN AGAIN, I CAN'T TAKE IT.

Howard was due to go out in the field for a week, and Brenda decided I'd stay with her. She knew how I was scared of staying alone at night. The next morning she asked me if I was having my periods regularly. Since my miscarriage, they never came regular anymore. When I asked her why, she said that I sure got up a lot in the night. I then put in a urine test and was surprised to find out I was pregnant. Part of me was happy and the other asked if it was going to happen again. I was still a bit scared of doctors and the test. Brenda had always taken me along to her appointments so I could watch the baby while she went in. I now know what she was trying to accomplish, and I'm glad I had such a good friend who cared. She was like my protective shield who wanted me to learn the world instead of letting it destroy me, because of my ignorance from living such a sheltered and secluded life for almost nineteen years.

Reading the books Brenda had given me made me better able to understand how my body was going to be changing. When Howard came home from the field we had decided to wait until I made it through my third month before telling anyone. I couldn't believe I could go through another miscarriage plus getting letters from back home saying how sorry they felt about it. We spent many times asking each other, will this one make it. Howard always made sure I had three square meals with plenty of fruits. Hawaii was the perfect place for that. The elderly lady in the apartment near us always deliver me bunches of bananas each week. She was Hawaiian and had her daughter bring some over every week.

After my third month was gone we called everyone back home to let them all know. They weren't too thrilled of the fact we waited to let them know, but we felt more at ease doing so. They were all happy for us.

When I called Mom to tell her, she was of course happy for us. She told me she would send me a picture she took of Patrick sleeping with the Easter basket I had sent him. Then she told me not to worry but Patrick was in the hospital with pneumonia. It wiped the joy inside of me out immediately. I felt so low the rest of the day I wished I had enough money to go home. Howard said he could get advance pay, but didn't think it was wise to do so in fear of the baby. It would take months to save the money for me to come back after paying the money back and keeping the rent. So instead, I kept calling home until he was just fine to me. He called for me Mom said many times. My stomach had been upset from the time I found out until he was in the clear. That was mostly the only time I really hated being on the island, other than being home sick and missing Patrick. Of course Christmas on the island seemed like such a fake set up with no snow.

There was always so many restrictions on the island. As military people we were able to go on base and sign out equipment for three days. All you would have to do is give them your ID card. The gyms were open for both men and women. One thing I found different was that the washers and dryers were left out in the open. Apartment people had them on their porches, some even without overhead protection. It was so hard to believe the climate out there. Sometimes it would rain on just one side of the street.

Some of the bingo games were played with gifts instead of money. There were weekly fund raiser games held at the same place each week. On Saturday night we would love to take a moon lit ride on the ferry to go play bingo on Fort Island. The ride on the ferry to go play bingo was so lovely. With the smell of fresh flowers in the air, the moonlight above you, and a peaceful sea breeze, we use to just look at the beautiful lights and mountains ahead of us. You could see so much at one time.

Since the climate there was always good you'd go to beach parties, and surfing was super because military men had to try everything. There would always be plenty of competition going on in all sports. Scuba diving was the only sport that had me on needles, since I never did learn to swim. When Howard would try that one I was always thinking he was under too long. That was the time I lost Howard's wedding ring, when he gave it to me while he went diving. When I bent over to pick up a shell, I dropped it and at the same time a big wave came in. It was gone in a flash. Howard, of course, was upset with me, but I promised to get a new one by doing some baby sitting to pay for it.

The most enjoyable time I had was when I was invited to a louou at the zoo. They loved to celebrate by doing it in style. It was the event of the kindergardeners that were graduating. They put on a big stage show for their parents and you should have seen the talent. They made it a whole day event. The kids were so filled with joy you could see how much love and support their parents were giving back. The buffet table was filled with so much, all was eaten by the end of the night. I was so honored to have been witness to such a beautiful performance.

The zoo was so big that it would take you two days to really see it all. They also had many famous ships you could visit and some redone into fancy dining rooms. They were so big with many historical items to see. You could also take a boat ride to visit the USS Arizona with the names of men who gave their lives to protect our land.

The Japanese also played a big part on the island, with their beautiful traditional style restaurants and food. I must say the food there was very tasty and so well spiced it was very easy to enjoy. They took a lot of pride in the way they cooked their food.

I remember one French restaurant we went to, I tried to speak French and realized how my French was slipping. We also found out after entering into the restaurant that we weren't dressed for the place. There wasn't anyone we knew there that spoke French, so my language was going down hill. Back home Mom always spoke French and we answered her in English. That's how Mom learned how to speak English. When we were younger all we could speak was French, so when we started school the older one's had to repeat first grade. Dad spoke both because he was partly raised in the city, so this helped us a little.

The fire on the desert was amazing at that French restaurant and so was the price, but it was good. I think that it was the most expensive place we ate at on the island. Some of the military people had their families go over to visit the island. It gave many of them the perfect opportunity to visit the rest of the family and see the island. We would pick some flowers and make them into lays. We all would get together and meet the people at the airport and celebrate all night. Out there you never went to bed early at night. To me the atmosphere helps to lift your spirits all the time. We always planned to visit the sugar cane fields and the pineapple fields. We also stopped at the sample stands on the way. We would plan a big beach party with plenty of competition in it, plus we all would collect a few poucka shell necklaces to take home with us. With the beach parties, sight seeing and shopping, they were always in hope to come back for more.

As far as for the cost of living, it wasn't as bad as I first thought. The rent is reasonable, and so was the cost of food. We had plenty of money to enjoy many of the finer thing on the island. The cost of clothing was the biggest saving because it was like only one season to buy for. In the winter months you may need a sweater on occasion.

When we first got there it seemed very hot to us. A few days later I couldn't stand it anymore, so I cut my hair to help cool me off.

The first time I started to miss the season back home was when our first Christmas came around. When we put up the tree, it felt like I was pretending to put on a show in the wrong season. It was strange to adjust to being able to shop on Sunday. The feeling of visiting on Sunday was gone, because back home week days was to work and Sunday was a day of rest. We went to church in the morning and then company came in the afternoon. All around it was better living there then back home. At home everyone was more interested in making more money then just having a good time, and living a relaxing life.

On nights that Howard would have to work late I would walk up the street and watch the little girls learn to houla. The whole front wall was glass so many people could stand there and watch them go at it. At times they would go to the malls to perform for the people who went shopping. That was a time to see them in the little dresses. For me it brought many memories back of my young dancing days. To think how little they were and dancing so cutely brought happiness to all.

When I was in my fourth month of pregnancy I began to worry again, because I hadn't felt the baby move. I wrote to my sister Lisa and asked her when the baby was supposed to move. I then talked to the doctor about it at my next appointment. He then asked me to ask my mother-in-law if she would send any information she could on Howards brothers. Because it being her first grandchild she got them to us immediately. I was in my fifth month before movement began, and our minds were put at ease again. I was feeling fine and things were going smoothly.

Howard of course was continuously spoiling me. We began to talk about choosing the name and setting rules on how we were going to raise our child. Howard was concerned mostly with making sure the child had the many things he never had. My concern was that they would never live such a secluded life. If they were old enough to ask a question I felt they would be old enough to get an answer from me. I hoped to keep an open relationship so if there were anything on their minds they would feel free to talk about it. Like most parents, we would talk about what they would like to be when they grew up.

When I was in my seventh month I began to feel so much pain so I immediately went to the hospital. They found out that I was having contractions and they gave me some pills to ease the pain. They also told me to go home and stay in bed, and if my water broke and I started to bleed to come in right away. When morning came the pain was still there, so Howard asked a neighbor to keep a close eye on me. When I went to my appointment the doctor explained the importance of staying in bed and that I really didn't want the baby now. So I went home to bed, and

Howard gave me magazines and a television in the bedroom. If I had to get up I would only need to go to the bathroom. He also would fix breakfast for me before he would go to work every morning. He paid a lady to come in and defrost the freezer and clean house. At noon time he would come home for lunch to see if I was getting some sleep and make sure I was alright.

This went on for five days when Howard decided to take his leave. The next morning as Howard was going out the door to go pick up his leave papers, I screamed to him. When he came in to find out what I wanted he just stood there looking at me. I told him to call the base and tell them that he was going to the hospital. I had started to spot some blood, and the pain was worse then it was the day before. I actually had to tell him what to do next. The man who was so calm, cool and collective just stood there.

When we arrived at the hospital they put me in a private room and hooked me up to all kinds of machines. They told me the machines would tell them every contraction that was made. They told me that some people miscarry in their third month and some have miscarriages in their seventh month. At first all I could do was cry, but I kept hearing the heartbeat and the baby kicking. I kept saying to myself it wasn't true and it can't be happening to me. Howard never said too much, he just held my hand and we kept looking at each other in silence.

Two hours later I went into full labor, and pain was harder and they were unable to give me any relief, because they had to make sure the baby would be awake when it was born. Three hours later I gave birth to a boy, he weighed three pounds and eleven ounces. December 12, 1974. At that time all they told me was his weight. Joy filled my heart to think I had given birth. I saw him briefly and I was very happy, but yet in my mind I knew he was very small, and there was a chance he wouldn't make it. I knew nothing about premature babies. Mom had once said

I came one month early and was five pounds and three ounces but I had never heard of anyone smaller. He was so tiny. While the doctors were finishing up with me. I asked him if the baby would be home for christmas. He told me he couldn't tell me the condition of the baby. They took him immediately up to the ward, to check him over, then came down to tell me that he wouldn't be home for christmas. If things were all right it would still take time to get him to the proper weight.

They then took me to the recovery room. I was starved and just in time for lunch. Half an hour later a priest came in to tell me he had given my baby his last rights. I began to get scared that he wasn't going to make it. Praying and begging God to save my baby was all I could do. The doctor came in a half hour later as I was still praying, and told me the baby had ten fingers and ten toes. Then he told me when the test they were running was done he would tell me more. The doctor said the baby was taken to the premature nursery and when I arrived to my room I could go see him.

A short time later I was taken to my room from recovery. Howard was back from eating, so we went to see the baby. We first had to scrub then put on some robes before we could enter the nursery. We were in total shock to see the baby all hooked up to all kinds of machines, and nothing but skin and bones. We just stared and prayed he would be alright. They came over and explained what each machine was used for. This lead us to believe he was much worse than we thought. The next day was even harder for us, because when we walked in there the baby was under a very hot lamp. He had caught yellow jaundice. The lamp was causing him to lose some of his weigh. When feeding time came I felt they were cruel to the baby when they put a plastic tube down his throat to feed him. First they had to empty what was left in his stomach from the last meal before putting in the new milk. They had told us he had trouble breathing the night before so they had to put this little cage over his head. We then were able to hold him briefly, with him being so small and all those machines hooked to him. We could only hold him for awhile so they could put him back under the lights.

A few days later they put him in a regular incubator without the light. He was able to put on a few ounces but before they would let him out he caught yellow jaundice again. So they had to put him back under the lights until it was gone completely. Again, he started losing weigh, but he no longer needed help breathing.

As the weeks went by the only problem he seemed to have was in gaining weight and we were confident he was going to make it alright. I began to go to the library to read up on premature babies, so I could know what it all meant. A lot of the words in the books were new to me, but Brenda was always there to explain them to me. By the time little Howard was four pounds six ounces and ready to come home I had a general idea of what to look for in case of trouble. He was put on a special formula which only came in powdered form.

The day they told us we could take him home, you should have seen us, we were like a couple of kids with a new toy. We called everyone back home to let them know, and they were so happy to see the baby made it. They hadn't given him much hope. Howard's mom had said she was afraid we were going to lose him when we had first called to tell her. Mom said they prayed every night that he would make it. Back home when relatives were in the hospital, we would all get together at night and pray they would be all right.

He was late on starting his shots but that was expected. At first he started having trouble keeping his formula down, so they trying different ones. At the hospital on base you always got a different doctors and that's cause a problem in junior's case. They would end up leaving me in the examining room to talk to other doctors who would change his formula. He had too much phosphate in his system which was why he could only be on this certain formula. From what I gathered, sometimes babies have too much but not at juniors level. He seemed to have fevers often that had no explanation at all which caused delay in his shots. This resulted in his starting his shots over again.

When he was three month old he started crying different in the middle of the night, so I immediately got up to find out he was spitting up blood. Howard was out on field training. I took him to the base doctor, and was told if he done it again or had blood in his bowels to take him directly to the hospital. By the time we got back home he started it again, so I called the hospital to let them know we were on the way in and what the base doctor had said. Junior just kept on having bloody musces over and over again. About every half hour. They would run all kinds of test on him. I also had to sign papers to let them take a spinal tap test. They had put him in critical condition and they continued to run tests but nothing was showing up wrong. He had lost all energy and they had to start him on an I V. They tied his hands down so he wouldn't pull the I V out when he was awake. All I could think is please God don't let me lose him , he's been the light of my life and I just couldn't lose him now. Praying was all I did that night till I fell asleep.

The next morning when I woke up I was angry to see they had shaved his head in the night and never woke me up, to put an I V in his head I felt they should have had my permission first before doing such a thing. I knew I would still have given my permission but I felt they still should have asked . He slowly began to recover and the cause of it was never found. Some say he was probably going to be one of those crib death babies. What ever the case I'm glad I acted fast on the sound of a different cry. Mothers day was the first holiday junior spent home with us. We started the day giving junior's Hawaii grandma a bouquet of flowers. She had given me my fruit all during my pregnancy and bought junior a scale when he was born, which was just what I needed for him. So we always called her that, and she was tickled to death by it. Howard took a picture of her with junior and the flowers for a keep sake for when we leave the island. Then we went on our first ride half around the island as a little family. We stopped at the milk farm and had lunch, then to the pineapple stands for a fresh cool drink. As we continued our ride around the outskirts of the island we also stopped to see the step by step raising of the sugar cane and pineapple fields. We also stopped and visited the Indian store to see all the beautiful items they made by hand. They put so much time in the making the items and so much of their tradition for you to see first hand. We also saw some straw huts on the ride which we had thought were only in the movies. Many of the entrances had big wooden faces which were high in size but very stylish. We ended the day with a cooked ham supper which Howard had prepared for me with flowers, While junior and I took a nap, a perfect end to a special day. After supper we talked about all we had been through since on the island to finally be Mom and Dad to enjoy this beautiful day.

Our two years on the island were coming to an end, and I was set to leave a month before Howard. Junior was find until the time came near, then he started to have problems in eating again, even throw he was six months old he was only allowed to have formula because his tube from his stomach to his intestines was not fully formed and we had to avoid the possibility of it getting plugged up. My ticket was paid for on one of those special flights for military people so if I was to cancel it, I would lose my money. They arranged to have junior examined the morning before we left and they gave me his records. So as soon as I arrived home I could take him to the base to be seen immediately.

The flight was long and hard with junior crying all the way. The stewardess helped out a lot by walking him and so did some of the people on the plane. The noise had scared him all the way, and we had many stops with long delays. When I finally arrived home they didn't even recognize me. The new grandma's were trying to pick me out from the crowd as we all got off the plane. Because I had gained so much weight they didn't even recognize me as I stepped off the plane with my child. Mom never though I'd ever gain weight that was a problem I always had growing up trying to gain. But it sure was a happy reunion, and it felt so good to be back home.

Junior had a bit of trouble in holding his formula down after the trip, and in Hawaii his formula could be bought at any drug store. But when we were at the doctors he asked me how much of it I had on hand because it was not common in the state. So I went to our town drug store and asked them if they could find some. They told me they would have to do some calling to see if they could track some down. The next day they called me back, and said they had found some but I had to buy the whole case. The Maine weather agreed with junior very well and when he turned a year old he was able to start eating baby food. Though he is still under weigh and short like his mother he has been doing fine.

SUMMARY

When I look back at my very modest up-bringing in Maine, how we were so sheltered from life out on the farm, where going to town to church was the big event of the week. I wish all those scary torments would have never been. The joy of having a child is so important, that fear shouldn't have interfered with the happiness of pregnancy. I wish I had never been brought up so modest and to have to go through all the experience I did. I think living on the farm taught us some values we need today, like good hard work is the only way to get ahead in life, but be sure to have respect for people along the way. But living on the farm in such a modest and secluded life has put me through so much hardship and loss that I may never be able to live free with it. I have tried to understand my life but at times I have hate inside at the way my parents brought me up. At times I blame them directly for the loss of my baby. It makes it hard for me to talk to them when knowing I'm feeling low. Knowing they have no idea what harm they have really done to me inside. They can't begin to see my loss. I'm still very close to Patrick and hurt deep inside whenever he has a problem and at times I get over sensitive. But I have been able to detach myself from acting and over protecting him like a mother. I feel having junior has helped me do so and hopeful time will heal the past.

About the Author

As more parents are choosing to home tutor there children for the good reasons, I found myself complied to write my true story to help parents understand the long lasting effect's of the modest shelter, upbringing before making the final decision. As a school volunteer I only wish for parents to see how a child maybe affected and that these issues also need to be addressed.